To order additional copies of this book, contact:
Xlibris
1-888-795-4274
www.Xlibris.com
Orders@Xlibris.com

Tales of Candyland

sweet but spicy

Candy

Contents

Your Love

Your love drives in pounding rain,

just to get to you,

She's your love who feels your pain,

she cries with you,

this love of hers will not wane,

she stays steadfast with you,

your love is genuine, you raise no Cain,

for that, she thanks you,

your love is patient, you wait for her, that sweet Jane,

she also waits for you,

your love to her is kind,

you send her flowers of not plain,

she knows the sweetness of you,

your love will endure and it will reign,

through thick and thin, you remain with her and she with you!

Sent from my iPhone

Time Spent Wasted

I shalt consider a futile moment whence I did matter to mine frenemies,

once we befriended only 'cause the situation couldeth not ignore it, time aged and we leaned to enemies,

we did share fate by chance!

Am I deserving to them a backward glance?

I changed, gaping past made us strangers,

gossiping words if I hated, doth make me a reputation danger,

history book pages flipped,

Facebook of yesterday-years I have a time or two dipped,

I still ponder,

Have I fallen into oblivion?

Unhappy thinking that I'd might matter, my mind doth wander,

Shake myself to the loose,

it would be better to coerce with a goose,

I'm wiser than a zygote,

I wit the difference betwixt myself and inanimate objects,

I not gloat,

people come, stay awhile and go,

in mine head, memories of so named friends stand before me as a folly show,

On and off button to my brain I lack!

Hast thou a toggle switch?

Reflecting I continually do whilst the past cometh back.

The Shepard Calls Unto Me

Santa is jolly,

the Bunny is cute,

the both, I put on mute,

good golly,

the Lamb of God,

lest we forget,

many shares this should get,

on the grassy hills of sod,

I shame not to carry the cross,

my feet may be sore,

my back twists, I roar,

i awake early from turn and toss,

I am no Queen Of Sheba rather just a child,

I dream of no Jacob's Ladder,

Devil or Jesus, I choose the latter,

the power of the Lord is great, evil is weak or mild,

keep your presents,

search not for the hidden eggs,

I walk to the Lord on my own two legs,

I rest now in the Shepard's presence!

Only An Imperfect Human

After the crime, the criminal returns,

not a question, the person of interest comes to relive,

they don't want to be a villain like in Batman Returns,

shocked now to be labelled forever a criminal, what can they give?

Truly sorry, I hope they'd be,

life throws things of disturbing circumstances,

a crime was committed, they hid like a sneaky dog flea,

redemption is available,

not all fall in this category,

send an apologetic note, make it mailable,

be real and sincere, a simple sorry'd suffice, don't need a lengthy story!

Lunch Pail Blues

Faded smiley face of a known hero that is far from zero,

plastered on my lunch box which I am crazy about like a fox,

it frowns when its inner becomes someone's dinner,

bullet shaped thermos contains no Noss,

too bad, I could in the class rule, suffer no loss,

dessert is a King Dong,

is this said above a character with a thong,

an apple to boot, probably not with the doctor in cahoots,

lunch pail of childhood reflecting,

a child as I was, never knew my future expecting,

Barbie Doll lunch box would have pleased me lots,

Incredible Hulk was my lunch pail hero,

high school was I with a paper lunch bag of not mucho dinero!

Pac Family

Chomps on the dots in her well known maze of many mazes,

the ghosts don't stand a ghost of a chance during their chase phases,

MsPacMan can pack it in and not gain a pound,

she already is a bit round in a round about way, moving without a sound!

She meets PacMan, a gluttonous fellow who also fights his battles with bulging eyes of coloured sheets,

PacMan likes his life simple, one maze is a good enough as he death cheats,

wears no makeup like MsPacMan does,

prefers to be fully plain just because,

he packs a punch when the ghosts turn blue from a power pellet which PacMan devours

when he's close to biting the bullet!

Once upon time in a hurry like a rushed order of a McDonald's mcflurry,

PacMan And MsPacMan meet and greet, chase and race,

exchange wet kisses from their yellow face,

they fall in love and take a break from the high scoring above!

One day, a baby comes along,

it didn't take long,

a stork brings Junior PacMan to the mix,

a quick little of about the age of six who runs like his parents in a huge maze that he finds himself in,

munching on the trails of some fine din din!

4 sets of ghoulish enemies for each Pac member, life is hard, always on the run,

ghosts are freaky and geeky, they follow each other every one,

hunt in packs and sometimes set traps,

they know the mazes like well rehearsed maps,

the PacMan trio, PacMan, MsPacMan and Junior PacMan are a famous 80s characters
like looney tunes, cereals named after them, posters, shirts and even funny cartoons,

Arcade games that stood the test of time and certainly one of my favourites all of all time!

Instead of big machines in the gaming stores,

I just sit and relax as I play my Pac family on my I phone, having fun as I try to gather some high scores!

If Pantyhose Could Squawk

They barely walk the walk,

if they could talk they'd squawk,

stretch they do,

I stretch the truth, I not do,

support the unmentionables,

I might flatulence commit, it'd be unintentional,

fake tans my beige pair could mimic,

pull up tight to avoid legs of elephant bulimic,

snag 'em not, then run the stockings won't,

watch your nails so they don't,

smooth legs I seek,

wearing pantyhose I feel not like a geek,

sheer energy I feel,

I wear my nylons with much appeal,

pantyhose actually expire,

reinforced panty and especially control top if you desire,

treat 'em well,

delicately wash by hand if they slightly smell,

hang to drip dry,

stockings last longer instead of early goodbye,

if pantyhose could squawk,

they'd tell ya all this said here-above,

so chalk it up, use a chalk!

Thus 't Varied

Fully, I miss thee to the none,

searing red metal wouldeth scorch mine hands,

shrivel doth my skin from damaging rays of tis sun,

braver to me that I let welcome heat to compass me about, mark me, I do speak of no shenanigans!

Partially, I speak of thee, thou reckless loon,

transport me to the ruddy Mars,

wherein breathe doth escape my lungs as the vacant air of the Moon,

I drink myself to an alcohol poison as such perilous fumes from exhaust pipes of cars!

Wholly, I am exempt from thee, wherefore hast thou hid from me?

A binding contract that hath assuredly been annulled,

thou flunkest a test, much folly in thee,

back to the creepy and dank crawl space from whence thou didst crawl!

Distant Friends/ Close Strangers

Saying hello is a chore,

too busy forevermore,

once excited to reconnect,

it had a special effect,

height of our togetherness,

glad or sad times, we shared nevertheless,

phoned or texted back and forth,

made plans and invited others and so forth,

time changes,

less and less a word exchanges,

saying hello feels distant,

how I long for a closeness this instant,

no goodbye is in my vocabulary,

I miss you my friend whom I a chance to see rarely!

I Bid Thee Ado But Bid Thee Well!

I tread without heed upon ambers of the fire pit,

I durst say that mine health doth matter zilch if thou dost not return unto me,

didst thou not say ofttimes for thy love endureth to end times?

Befuddled brain remaineth in me,

I do commit myself to this with a sheepish smile,

if thou speakest with a false tongue, then may thine head be separated from off thy shoulders,

I shalt not be mocked!

Beguilest me thrice,

before my friends, I was made a fool, I shalt shake thee off like a loosened fall leaf,

let thyself be scarce from me,

methinks that I be too ignorant at times,

a be-drenched dog wit not the mess that it hath made,

a weaning babe hath care of nought but the milk,

anon, I became wiser liken unto graduated medicine man,

an elephant never forgets, an idiom I oft hearken,

I wish thee an happier life with thy next endeavour,

may a bless'd woman find favour in thy sight!

Beknownst To Selfe

Thou hearkenst unto me as I divulge,

I say with all candour,

I heere me,

betwixt' mine heart n' opaque head,

tis door of metal bee fain closed,

wherefore doe I permit a crass society to make me mad?

a time, gluttonous heart hath made it selfe merry,

open mind didth segregate nought,

anon, I beleeve I am bereft of

normalcy,

be thou of a surety that I shall live as a recluse til I let go of the futile past,

lo, thou hadst been a long time friend, I wot not what 'd do without thee,

tarry for me a fortnight, I press my lips shut, no more words do I utter!

I heere me, only my selfe conscious doth reiterate my anguish!

An Ordinary Day To Me

Sun bleached hair,

blue white striped t shirt to wear,

white socks with blue tennis shoes to match,

I sit on a grass hill patch,

waiting for my date in his frilly dress,

he found the idea from his app. of spring outfits on Pinterest!

I'm an independent girl who's fond of wearing dark blue dressy jeans,

I set the mood and the blanket for a picnic as the sun above sends its beams,

my pretty boy comes with white feminine flats,

bronzed face and touch of makeup to go with that,

white stockings and a summer dress with a fedora,

he looks picturesque like a little girl sitting in an atrium with surrounding flora,

not a care in the world do we have,

a few may laugh, feel disgusted or hurt, here some salve,

to each his or her own,

let it alone,

dresses are cute!

Nothing nice to say? Keep it at mute,

I love me and my boy loves his outfit,

I accept different, i won't throw a fit!

Benchmark

I sat straight up on a wooden bench,

hoping that I didn't give off much stench,

police officer walked on by,

nodded his head as he readjusted his fly,

I laid back down,

I was a hobo without the makeup of a clown!

Before I returned to sleep,

I saw a black purse on the ground, should I snatch it to keep?

Lots of money inside,

I ran with it to the officer, I did decide,

'cause of my good nature, I was awarded at the police station,

a lady who lost her purse gave me a job at the nearby shelter, plus I received a letter of citation!

Many a times as a I sat on the old bench with hands interlaced,

I used to pray for a miracle that I could be of service to the human race,

I lived on a park bench without my name inscribed on it,

now, an award for citizen of the year was much more meaningful with a job to go with it!

Rain On The Rake

My house is not big at all but rather small,

my rake is stored in my spare bedroom along the wall,

roof is leaking, stains give proof when water does fall,

floor gets wet, I get upset, my tears are raw!

Warts from worrying, thoughts are stirring, my life is dull,

lay-off come and go, money disappears before you know, I feel the fall!

I used to rake in the cash, a healthy stash but now my rake rusts
from the attic rain, drip by drip, it starts off small,

I need a fresh start in order to buy food from the produce mart, no shopping for me at the Mall!

My phone rings, I pretend not to hear a ting, bill collectors continue to call,

I'm not ready to be raked over the coals, I want to make some
goals like climb over the prison of my four walls,

I can sell my only tool the old rake, rusty and wood soaked, not sure of the model
or make, life will turn around, prayer works, I say with a lot of gall!

Made Of Dishonour

Me is first 'cause I for money athirst,

you be second, you are not that important, me a reckon,

mine is mine for all time being,

I a selfish human being,

me is high, you be low, I lead, you follow in toe,

look at me, I shine under the spotlight with smug glee,

look at thee, you with second hand clothes, I better, hear ye, hear ye,

cruel am I? Care factor far from high,

I am rich and arrogant but can't find a hitch,

you seem glad, not at all mad,

more friends than I ever had,

money tree I shake, me sly like a snake,

family tree you make, in you love is real, you no fake!

Made Of Dishonour

Me is first 'cause I for money athirst,

you be second, you are not that important, me a reckon,

mine is mine for all time being,

I a selfish human being,

me is high, you be low, I lead, you follow in toe,

look at me, I shine under the spotlight with smug glee,

look at thee, you with second hand clothes, I better, hear ye, hear ye,

cruel am I? Care factor far from high,

I am rich and arrogant but can't find a hitch,

you seem glad, not at all mad,

more friends than I ever had,

money tree I shake, me sly like a snake,

family tree you make, in you love is real, you no fake!

Gravy In Bread Will Sink!

Smile real like Grimace after McDonalds stayed open late,

dial not the rotary phone after bed time, girl with big hair and I have a date,

file under phoney, scam exists over the phone,

while I rode as a kid, the plastic pony, parent was there, I, not alone,

mile I walk, unpaid bill of cell,

style of modern, I dressed to impress, not me but I unique wagon fell,

Nile I swim, a chance of wall to reach,

birds and bees, I, from no one, had the proper teach!

Noodle Dangly

My soup noodle, I slip and slop,

al dente on the floor it flops,

lying listlessly, an albino tapeworm it represents,

an infested fowl, dirty birds of pheasants,

white noodle without a tan,

white rice is its biggest fan,

Uncle Ben would be proud,

rice and noodle in Campbell's soup du jour if allowed,

I, the floor eventually mop,

noodle in the garbage pail I let it drop,

white rice, a mitochondria as a coated pill misses white noodle of no gender,

trash with the rest of the cast, you find the dropped noodle bent like a metal of fender bender!

The Eyes Have A Part

I shut mine eyes,

darkness me it despise,

dizzy from scared nothing,

answer is a coffin?

I go the way when God is ready,

til' then I am on full tilt, I keep me steady,

scared of the moon,

tomorrow will eventually be noon,

afraid to continue,

depression take a hike, please discontinue,

love is in me 'cause Jesus is there,

miracles exists, God loves without prejudice, that is fair,

I make myself glad with next day open minds eye,

thank you Lord of hosts, before thee, I am not experiencing shameful cry!

Elf Is Not On His Shelf

Elf is keeled over in the drawer,

too much Irish whiskey the night before,

Mrs. Elf is beyond furious,

he drives her oh so delirious,

long time not on the shelf,

dust gathers like interests for the wealth,

no more drinking for Mr. Elf,

New Years resolution he promised unto himself,

baby elf on the way,

quickly comes that day,

Elf sits on his shelf for to be ready

as though waiting for money to be owed to him by a friend named Teddy!

University Scare

Grounds of learning,
knowledge I'm yearning,
campus of pompous,
sidewalks of high flown pimples of puss,
broke to gain a degree,
loans pile up like a dog of pedigree,
books to be used barely,
soon to the used section unfairly,
borrowed money,
parents rich to help their honey,
school and work,
work and school, go berserk,
no promise of a ready to steady careers,
bank called, you are already in arrears,
year 1, like the course,
year 2, change the major, of course!
University is scary,
to graduate is almost contrary.

Dead On His No Foot

Ghost of a chance,

takes a quick glance?

voice too misty to say boo,

failed before, nothing new,

Halloween is here,

motivation without fear,

two women walking down the street,

behind the bushes, he will them meet,

comes out to scare,

the ghost's cover sheet is a snare,

his bare bones are truly shown,

the two ladies laugh but soon groan,

half of his body is missing,

the ghost explains as they quietly listen,

his front looks like a fender bender

'cause he is a transgender member

and half of his body is only there,

due to the surgery costing the ghoul an arm and a leg to cover his share!

Picky Esther W/ Liquid Gesture

Finland is where I go for din din,

hungry like a wolf, I laugh like a hyena, I eat pie only with cinnamon,
Hungary is not along a gulf, i geography not well, where is Regina?

Rockies is where I go to drink on the rocks, thirsty as a baby with baby bottle, I
chug like a 350 carburetor, I can drink alone if music rocks off my socks, water,
water everywhere but not a drop to drink, water enough for an alligator!

> Dead On His No Foot

>

>

> Ghost of a chance,

> takes a quick glance?

> voice too misty to say boo,

> failed before, nothing new,

> Halloween is here,

> motivation without fear,

> two women walking down the street,

> behind the bushes, he will them meet,

> comes out to scare,

> the ghost=E2=80=99s cover sheet is a snare, his bare bones are truly

> shown, the two ladies laugh but soon groan, h

In The Worth

My thin grass of much patch,

I rip my toupee off to leave a thatch,

astro turf do the trick,

transplant my hair with a pick,

fake plants and flowers cover my indoors,

antique lantern burns within an ol' log cabin indoors,

save the water, no mess on the floor from the tropics,

save the heat, no high bill to make one sick,

used lawnmower clinking and clanking,

rotten railroad ties outside the border of bushes flanking,

rows of cut grass in the front a beauty,

evergreen trees and perennials overrun the edges of the house and trim, they do their duty!

A Time When I Was A Nothing

When I belittled me,

lower than the abyss of a salted sea,

worth the clothes on my back,

get off my back, I said truly, Jack!

took lots of courage mustered,

proud of me would Mr. Custard,

grade school not end quickly,

now I'm reminiscing, my head filled with it profusely, younger tight mind and squeezed years, too me to show the real me, I reserved tears, brain washing escape my better half, I old enough to do my own wash, older than a powdered milk fed calf, I was a girly girl, I cried, I escaped any whip of a curled whirl, my blankets cover half of me, my white socks of ankle cuffs cover my fantasy legs of glee, I sure am, I can be myself, I sure bet you, I not on a lam, I like the attention but keep thine hands unto thyself!

Wise Words Of Endeavour

My head, the info is being in me fed,

I'm inundated with useless stuff, I need a shed, my winter joys are
next to my winter sled, I fast not but I observe instead!

Christmas I know the true winter purpose, stores are well equipped with junk surplus, I
thought, my thoughts are not to absorb self gain, I no stoic but I feel myself the lingering
bane, presents scattered, to and fro, my brain battered, who really cares, shmo?!?

Our suffer a little one, almost a party of restrained fun, Jesus, I praise thee and thy name
is capitalized, thou art bigger than the sun, if you are lucky enough, a next time does
still exist, a moment to thank the Lord and the hate is another time at a desist!

Hurry To Live

Such a hurry,

no time for a fast food Mcflurry,

such a hurry,

can not afford to be late, I worry,

such a hurry,

no time to enjoy lunch at work, back to the line, I scurry, be quick, I go to bed, the clock does tick, be quick, I can not afford less sleep, I get sick, be quick, one more show to watch, tv remote I click, slow down, I am already wound, slow down, one step at a time, no running around, slow down, police car hiding behind a sign, I found!

In A Non-Farmer's Field

I rose above the rubble,

a rose petal fell in the stubble,

my right arm too weak,

left arm still on the seek,

for the bandaid that fell off my head,

I dizzy, thin and thinking of Lizzy, I'm dripping red, a few fellow soldiers found their 2nd home, no fighting or angry animals to roam, others made the grade, families awaited, kids of the elated and wives that stayed, I saw a four leaf clover, I prayed for the war to be over, this field of nobody's dream, pits of soiled bullets, I wore a metal mullet, holes like moon craters, I a lucky one, I can safely say, see ya later!

Ich Werd' Gerettet

Selig bin ich, jedes Mal ich meinen Herr andenk', fertig bin ich, wenn er mich zu Hause anruf', glücklich fühle ich mich, daß ich nicht vergessen wird, Gott gab uns Leben und der Herr will uns wahrhaftig es halten!

Frei bin ich, wenn ich den Herr such',

irgendwo sah ich das in einem Buch,

sicher fühl' ich mich, wenn ich an den Herr vertrau'

dies Gefühl bleibt in mir und immer dauert, zufrieden bin ich, daß ich nie vorn dunkeln Angst hab', das Licht kommt zu mir, ich fall herab, Ich tu' weh, der Herr rettet mich, jetzt bin ich nicht allein, ich werd' gesegnet reichlich!

On Vous Écoute!

Il est ouvert la porte,

le monstre lui attendait en silence,

Andy ne pouvait pas voir dans les oubliettes, soudain, la créature lui attrapa par le bras mais Andy tomba dans un lac et puis il se réveilla de son lit très trempé, il humide le lit parce que le cauchemar était horrible!

Son père a dit à Andy qu' un film avant de se coucher peut causer des mauvais rêves et Andy était trop jeune pour regarder tels programmes.

Il faut comprendre que les adultes savent plus de temps ce que ses enfants ont besoin et ne voulent que de les protéger de danger!

Kimberley

Kimberley gets up and puts on

Ripped jeans that she forgot to mend,

she takes in the warm weather of the beautiful long weekend, She waltzes about gingerly, eats her gingerbread at the local eatery, a day off from work, Kim fills her coffee to the rim, strolls through the woods, she acts on a whim, on the Ganatchio Trail, she bikes along, humming to a tune of a classic song, don't call Kimberley to come in for overtime, she's enjoying a Corona on the beach with extra lime, a long overdue vacation is what her doctor ordered, now, Kim is well rested and in a better state of mind, sort of?!?

Time To Care

I am taking time to care for my Mother,

from one month to another,

I rest from work,

I stress out more and I hurt,

my mommy sacrificed hard and was there for me, now I am here for her as long it needs be, time eats away and the world turns under our feet, time well spent, making new memories that we so dear keep, I return one day to my tedious job in the factory, I count my blessings to have employment and a house of my own, yes siree but my mom is so special, kind and near to my heart, I just say thanks to all the wonderful Mothers who loved us kids right from the start!

Scary 'Cause No Drug!

A face of a bolt pattern on the centre of a 1950's tractor rim, sort of glim, chainsaw teeth of metal mouth and an alien antenna protruding thereat, it wasn't Sim, unpainted hoe handle legs, bell bottom cut as shorts, not fit for even Kim, tumble weed hair stiff but together like a rolled up barb wired fence of old school farming, she looks as my Aunt Mim!

I calls the shots, my mind is set on dim, I like her to the moon, my Aunt but stingy, my coffee is never to the rim, the imagination of mine runs rampant, weird thoughts not evil, not like her or him, my face and hair are not perfect, I am faulty too, myself has choice words, just ask Tim!

Whirling Dervish

Spinning like spinning tops,

shapes of shaker salts of mystifying dance, Turkey is the home of this popular move if one should at a map take a glance, getting closer to God is the purpose of this unique twirl, moving against the wind to dance is a oh negative like a inert whirl, feeling one with the creator is essential to the being, removing the black garb, the Turkish dancers are separated from the earthly things, believing is feeling, when one whirls, all the particles within the Earth flow along with a Whirling Dervish, a respected art form which is learned and performed by some people of the Turkish!

Content I Am

Guys are misters,

Girly I am, self in me contained,

I have rather hang with the sisters,

Unmanly men, I thrill to accompany,

No too many a crowd, two, three or four is a company!

With artsy side of humans is where you'd find me, I'm attracted to
open minded and creative thinkers, what think ye?

Feminine world I belong to,

Makeup, accessories and costumes you will find me there too!

Guys and gals of my artistic domain,

those are the ones that'd get my silly ideas, I know no plain, My friends of other smarts, I hold
dear as well, they accept me, we support each other even if the other a time that one fell!

Timothy's

Timothee is not spelled like thee,

at the first, he was she but not if ignorant doth someone be, blood flows through the veins, fluidity of gender now, say unto they or it howbeit this one shalt reign!

Respect the ground that yieldeth fruit,

trash it not,

respect Timothy, is this person less than the ground where dirt doth rest thereupon? I wit that thou wouldest think it not!

Partner it hath found,

au natural or with makeup,

be of good cheer and refrain from a wrongful noun, A judge who is omnipotent hath the better seat to label, Timothy findeth grace of the almighty and among people, love is love hath he spoken with a righteous tongue from the which he was able!

An Introduction To Destruction

A broke open King Dong strewn all the ploughed field, hoary frost like cotton ripped from a victim's shirt as he tried to yield, the smoke shack turned into a shocked shack, empty cans of spray may explode, watch it Jack!

Read the instructions!

Blood like tomato paste plastered on his pants, rotten tomatoes demolished, they bring about hungry ants, a sign blows rapidly in the harvesting wind, factory warns as it clinks and clangs of an ear shattering din!

Throwing tomatoes results in payroll deduction!

Cytoplasmic mucous surrounds the inert berry of jello, cellulite excess cut from an inexperienced surgeon, the poor bleeding fellow, infected wounds, bacteria cultured like cheese spreads on the skin, antibiotics comes quickly herein, make it thick and not thin!

The dream seemed real or was it rather an alien abduction?

Paper Issue

Kleenex box out of tissue,

that's my issue,

sweat from my curvy brow,

drops like holy water, holier than thou, a smeared painted face, no paper to make chase!

No name brand would do,

Kleenex back up to pick up poo,

3 ply sheets,

soft for my pedicured fetish feets,

my nose runs and very seldom bleeds,

Kleenex tissue in my purse,

in my pocket I pick, I have needs!

Paper towel too rough,

no guff,

skin so sensitive, so tender,

off to the store, I send myself,

about to sneeze, where's my cotton defender?

Bird And Crow

Eating like a bird,

crow's feet at the corner of the eyes,

starve yourself not, a bird's brain have you, don't be absurd, squint less and
moisturize the face, be smooth like crow's black dyed face and eyes!

A bird is still a word,

my head hurts like a crowbar to my noggin, no lying eyes, a
quick bird bath, ready to rest in my nest, word!

A crow eats a leftover corn cob on the window sill as I shut my tired eyes!

Don't Get Me Started!

Ether assist,

starts my engine,

I need assist,

sluggish I chug my gin,

day of no another dollar,

house cleaning a must,

check my phone for a caller,

time to gather some dust,

hungry like a neglected wolf,

attach my seatbelt, I not dog it, more of a fast paced wolf, house clean as of now, big chore finished in my home, a happy farmer's field done w/ a plough, evening time, things slow down, I still roam, I did dig fun, deserving after work is completed, I even changed my stockings that had a run, I muse often of past fun and of the contemporary bliss is celebrated!

Sealed But Not Forgotten

Deep in mind,

cabins of not disturbed,

a time set to march and a time to rewind, I thought of no one miss, history from a few perturbed, I remember and I like to reminisce, not forgotten, I still dare to care, some move on, bygones are long gone, my experiences, I am willing to share, I only wish to catch up from new but now ol' friends, you are new and not a forgotten song, be not afraid if I a friendly message your way send!

Couch Of Listen

Sit my end down,

I listen, help me, I'm down,

frozen with fear, my dear,

encouraging words, I hold so dear,

empty space before me,

trail I take, fork in the road, where is me?

I scare easily, I feel a wimp,

comes to me quite easily,

no strength to stand,

what to say, I make no stand?

attached to past security,

parents and old students are my security, change of scenery befits me not,
I fit in a band, circle of company, without it, I am nought!

Thus 't Varied

Fully, I miss thee to the none,

searing red metal wouldeth scorch mine hands, shrivel doth my skin from damaging rays of tis sun, braver to me that I let welcome heat to compass me about, mark me, I do speak of no shenanigans!

Partially, I speak of thee, thou reckless loon, transport me to the ruddy Mars, wherein breathe doth escape my lungs as the vacant air of the Moon, I drink myself to an alcohol poison as such perilous fumes from exhaust pipes of cars!

Wholly, I am exempt from thee, wherefore hast thou hid from me?

A binding contract that hath assuredly been annulled, thou flunkest a test, much folly in thee, back to the creepy and dank crawl space from whence thou didst crawl!

Short Supply

Short of patience, me flip me lid,

I am the shorter than most kids,

made no enemies once upon a phoney life, escaped trouble to please authority and any strife!

short of tolerance, me no inner strength, kept gossip at an arms length, less guts than a jelly box fish, to cancel a class speech, I could only wish, a quiet one, not much hand to raise to answer, quieter than a stealthy turtle or a ballet dancer, short of self assurance, shorter than a house's foundation, me with base or self identity, lack of foundation, worthy of nothing, self worth as zombie dead, sweet as a sweet doughnut but easily blush to full red, friends, I am lucky, me adorable as a rubber ducky!

My Chick O' Be

Chickadee,

I prithee,

give thee in, I am with thee not she,

methinks thou be not of a surety,

mine house from Surrey,

empty it doth sit, come thither aside me!

Chickadee,

thou seest me, thine eyes shine brightly, if I be beside me, thou quickenest thyself unto me, lo, behold, our hands interlaced by the sea, I bare my bare feet 'nt the sand, mine not much clammy, Chickadee, I prithee, anon thou comest in a haste not, before thee, I prepare some tea, I wit the spices therein, they do please thy tongue, my sweetie, set thee down at the table there about, relate a story for me, on the morrow, let us go we, to make a bond of marriage amidst friends in the city!

Mine Heart Valve Flutters

I trout not wherefore mine heart doth drain tis liquid love from therein!

Casserole juice hath an easy path to the wont, care of rubbish to nil, I live for good, I am of a worthy chap, methinks the love churning in mine organ chamber hath need of rescue, remainest thou not?

I occupy a moment of angst,

in the latter, 't shall pass,

wouldeth 't to thee that mine heart be made void of fertilizer of blood?

Thine head mayeth be light as a frayed feather, I wilt not be cut asunder as thou seekest hurt unto me!

Laugh Inward

Smile is a smile outwardly,

hurt is inside, I know not what maketh me cowardly, I don't want to be a stuck in the mud, I never try to act as the stud, me girl inside, struggles to genuinely smile outward, too much pressure, I might become fit for the straight jacket ward, I take lots, lot is full of cheap shots, jokes take i in stride, I let 'em ride, I smile but insult me friends not, I hate war but this battle I have fought, I protect my own, my friends, I not disown!

An Ordinary Day To Me

Sun bleached hair,

blue white striped t shirt to wear,

white socks with blue tennis shoes to match, I sit on a grass hill patch, waiting for my date in his frilly dress, he found the idea from his app. of spring outfits on Pinterest!

I'm an independent girl who's fond of wearing dark blue dressy jeans, I set the mood and the blanket for a picnic as the sun above sends its beams, my pretty boy comes with white feminine flats, bronzed face and touch of makeup to go with that, white stockings and a summer dress with a fedora, he looks picturesque like a little girl sitting in an atrium with surrounding flora, not a care in the world do we have, a few may laugh, feel disgusted or hurt, here some salve, to each his or her own, let it alone, dresses are cute!

Nothing nice to say? Keep it at mute,

I love me and my boy loves his outfit,

I accept different, i won't throw a fit!

Fudge Safe City

I wear my bars proudly,

I smack my chocolate bars loudly,

calm and proud,

excitable and loud,

defend my home land,

sweets make me hyper, 'tis a m&m man,

serious when I must,

spin my tires in the dust,

live in a country of freedom,

I chew the fat with mouth full of sugar gum, mam or sir, soldier of war, chocolate campaign, I support school programs whatever for, I wear a shawl or a bikini 'cause I'm allowed, trick or treat to kids or a large crowd!

I drive to a border of no wall,

marathon was the biggest candy bar I ever saw, I stand for thee, Canada, home sweet home, savour the flavour, sista and brotha!

He Chose!

The ripest in the case,

fresh and juicy without chemical lace,

I young but not forever, a fact I face, still love me? Would you to me make chase?

I not perfect, a past, I pardoned for erase!

never a bully, nor needed a can of mace, me is quiet, obedient and hugged one, not a basket case, take my time, enjoy life without a rat race, chose me? Be sure!

I left a mark, bread crumbs to trace,

I'm talented in my field, weird quirks, I am a confident ace!

Care about people I do, I set nobody abase, life is not easy, I try to keep a steady pace!

Benchmark

I sat straight up on a wooden bench,

hoping that I didn't give off much stench, police officer walked on by, nodded his head as
he readjusted his fly, I laid back down, I was a hobo without the makeup of a clown!

Before I returned to sleep,

I saw a black purse on the ground, should I snatch it to keep?

Lots of money inside,

I ran with it to the officer, I did decide, 'cause of my good nature, I was awarded at the police station,
a lady who lost her purse gave me a job at the nearby shelter, plus I received a letter of citation!

Many a times as a I sat on the old bench with hands interlaced, I used to pray for a miracle that
I could be of service to the human race, I lived on a park bench without my name inscribed on
it, now, an award for citizen of the year was much more meaningful with a job to go with it!

Picture Is Tilted

Shoulders of even,

head is leaning even,

even as Steven and straight as a arrow,

I duck not like a sparrow,

I see things at a different angle,

I learn more about the world, I attempt to ingest the U.S. star spangle, tilt my head and empty any high strutting ways, far from perfect, I not always spending time with my mind in a haze, I weak too, I support myself, friends are required, can't make it through by myself, I on full tilt, lowered myself off the stilts, base of better face, people fill my void space!

Grumpy

Grumpy sleeps in a bed of quite lumpy,

holes in his socks, cold floor, his apartment is run down, almost dumpy,

2 litre empty pop bottles and strewn on the floor some chips of Humpty Dumpty, he couldn't the rent anymore and told to leave but he felt warm and comfy, Grumpy got an idea and called the nearest shelter for the homeless on the street named Rumfy, the shelter took him in and rent was covered plus food was supplied by Rumfy and Umfy, a non profit place for the needy like Grumpy and his new friend Crumbly!

Sometimes In Another Time

Perturbed at this moment,

what a waste at a valuable time,

even if it be a time of lament,

I could have called to say I'm sorry when it was only a dime, time is rent-less, cares not, space I occupy, I shy of perfect, time fills any lot, I used to slave myself in trying to be perfect, failure was no option, don't enter, won't accept loser, my mind said I was at least existing in small caption, drugs I avoided, how degradable, I then never was a boozer, couldn't afford to be even less, life was weird but I had to work on the farm, we farmed, I had responsibilities, I confess, childhood okay, please don't worry, no cause to be alarmed!

Printed in the United States
By Bookmasters